UNDERSTANDING
Revelation 19

Victory over
One-World Government and
One-World Religion

Frank N. Mitchell

This UNDERSTANDING booklet is part of a series of booklets on key issues of our time on the Reign of Christ at
www.ashiningcityonahill.org
www.reignofchrist.org
All booklets are available at amazon.com

September 2018

UNDERSTANDING
Revelation 19
Victory over One-World Government and One-World Religion

Revelation 19 with its various prophecies may be the most controversial and debated chapter in all of the Bible. It is about Christ and the saints coming to Earth from heaven to defeat the demonic spiritual forces of the bad guys, so to speak, and they do this just after having had the Marriage Supper of the Lamb earlier in the chapter, and the chapter ends with Christ in the saints and the saints in Christ getting a massive victory, after which Satan is bound and Christ and the saints set up the thousand year Reign of Christ on planet Earth.

The Controversies of Revelation 19
Where do the controversies arise about this seemingly straightforward chapter? There are in the history of the Church basically three ways of looking at chapter 19 of Revelation.

First, there is common view often associated with amillennialism that says everything in Revelation, including chapter 19, has already happened in the early years of the Church. In fact, these people tend to believe that *all* Bible prophecy was completely fulfilled in the early years of the Church, and the Church Age is all that we are going to get of the Kingdom of God come on earth in all its fullness, and the next thing to happen is Christ returns and there is a Final Judgment and we go into eternity.

This view is almost self-evidently false because of the great violence it must do to countless prophecies that have yet to be fulfilled concerning the Kingdom come on earth and other matters and to prophecies that are fulfilled long after the early years of the Church, such as the Jews returning to Israel and reestablishing that nation.

If amillennialism is false, this leaves two other views concerning Revelation 19: one view is Christ and the saints literally and physically come riding out of heaven on physical horses in order to secure the planet from demonic control and from the one-world government and one-world religion that has taken over planet Earth, or a second view is Christ and the saints literally, but only spiritually, come from heaven, with the riding on physical horses being a symbolism of a literal spiritual reality that is taking place when Christ in the saints and the saints in Christ take on and defeat the demonically inspired one-world government and one-world religion that has taken over planet Earth.

In my personal opinion, for a host of reasons, it is the second of these two views that is quite literally the case in the realm of the spirit. In fact, there is no question about it; we are **not** going to be riding out of heaven on physical horses, please. I discuss this whole matter somewhat at length in the booklet

"UNDERSTANDING All Bible Prophecy." For our purposes here, the key to seeing that the riding out of heaven on physical horses is symbolic language of a spiritual reality is to see that the United Nations is without question the end-time one-world government of Babylon. For more on this see the booklet "UNDERSTANDING Globalism."

Further, the World Council of Churches and Vatican II are without question the apostate Church or Whore of Babylon of Revelation with their phony one-world religion. Once one can see these two facts concerning Babylon and the Whore of Babylon, seeing the riding out of heaven on physical horses as symbolic imagery and language follows fairly easily.

Why is this? Well, think about it. Here we are. We officially have had all the nations of the world foolishly embrace and commit to the United Nations Charter and the Universal Declaration of Human Rights, which are just an open rehash of the book *The New World Order* by H. G. Wells. That book in 1940 was a blueprint for a one-world socialist government to control all aspects of our lives and all aspects of the economy worldwide, and almost the only bad guys in Wells' New World Order were traditional Christians and traditional Jews, said Wells himself! And it was the highly and tragically confused Franklin and Eleanor Roosevelt who championed and implemented this outrageously evil and false vision for the world for the coming millennium in establishing the United Nations.

The United Nations, the World Council of Churches, and Vatican II

H. G. Wells was a socialist-democrat, "third-way" non-violent communist who in his book *The New World Order* outlined a utopian one-world communist government for the next millennium that would end all nation-states, all borders, all armaments, all capitalism, all private property and all free enterprise and that would end all traditional individual rights for new phony positive human rights, thus creating the political Babylon of Revelation to control all economics, thought, speech, education and so forth, and this was all openly so as the foundational purpose of the United Nations that all the nations of the world endorsed and committed to.

And in a similar manner, if you read the literature in and surrounding the World Council of Churches and Vatican II it is extremely clear that those Christians wanted to assert a new "Christianity." That new "Christianity" added to traditional Christianity the false idea that Christ supposedly died on the Cross to reconcile mankind to himself and not to God as in traditional Christianity. And that new "Christianity" added "the universal fatherhood of God and the universal brotherhood of man" to traditional Christianity in order to promote the one-world socialist agenda of Wells, FDR, and the United Nations, which is also based on the false morality of the universal brotherhood of man in order to do worldwide Social Justice, thus making these apostate mainline denominations the Whore of Babylon of Revelation, and this is not even a close call.

The point here is the utopian one-world socialist government of the United Nations to do worldwide Social Justice to make us all equal and to end any and all Liberty and Justice for anyone was a really, really, really stupid idea of the highest order, and it is without any question a demonic deception, a doctrine of devils, and a false good, but by 1948 all the nations of the world had bought into this outrageous demonic nonsense of the United Nations for whatever the reasons, and here we are.

In a similar manner, when the mainline Christian denominations of the World Council of Churches decided to add the clearly apostate universal fatherhood of God and universal brotherhood of man to the Christian faith along with the notion that Christ died on the Cross to reconcile mankind to himself, this was also a really, really, really stupid idea of the highest order, and it is also without any question a demonic deception, a doctrine of devils, and a false good, but virtually all of the mainline denominations of the world bought into it for whatever the reasons, and here we are.

The two major issues of our time: one-world government and one-world religion
What is the importance of this? The two major issues of our time are these two specific things. One is

tyrannical globalist government to control all nations, economic activities and every aspect of every person's life throughout the world, and the second is phony one-world religion to worship the non-existent God of all religions, which in fact is ultimately no more than a demonic spirit called Lucifer, the angel of false light, otherwise known as Satan, the demonic adversary of all mankind and of God's people in particular.

I think it is probably fair to say that since the 1960s things in this world and on planet Earth are not going too well since almost all political leaders of the world have, incredibly, embraced the utopian and globalist one-world tyrannical government agenda to do worldwide Socialist Justice to make us all equal that is proclaimed by the United Nations, while most Christian leaders of the mainline denominations of the world in their confusion have embraced a Lucifer worship of the false light of agape love as lawlessness, tolerance, inclusion, and religious ecumenicalism. After the UN was founded most churches added to their religious confusion the globalist agenda of international Social Justice and/or international-corporation globalism, and here we are.

These things are now the practical and official positions of governments and churches throughout the world. It is not as if Babylon and the Whore of Babylon of Revelation might happen or are about to happen. **They are a done deal actively playing**

themselves out, and they have been for the most part for a good 60 or 70 years.

There are and have been only two groups of folks protesting any of this, and they are generally considered to be either politically incorrect outcasts or deplorable Christian fundamentalists. That is, they are the people who have either not lost all common sense and still believe in free sovereign states, *or* they are Bible-believing Christians who have not bought into the Great Apostasy of Christian Liberalism, which has no real atoning work of Christ and promotes only a false agape love, utopian selfless service, and the Socialist Justice agenda of the socialist globalists with their phony baloney positive human rights to an equal share of the world's wealth.

The central message of Revelation:
The Final Victory
There is a central message to the book of Revelation, and that message is at the end of the Church Age a demonically inspired tyrannical one-world government is going to team up with a demonically inspired phony baloney one-world religion and take over planet Earth. Hello! It's a done deal! Wake up, smell the coffee!

This, in fact, is the post World War II world that most people alive today were born into, and this well-established and well-entrenched system of demonically inspired world government and world religion is now a given on planet Earth, and it will continue to be unless and until some people rise up to reestablish free sovereign states as the point of good government as well as reestablish traditional Bible-based Christianity as the point of all religion. It is not just apostate Christians who are literally worshipping (false-light) demons; **all** other religions outside of true Judaism and Christianity are literally, not figuratively, worshipping demons as well.

In this context the meaning of Revelation 19 is pretty obvious. At some specific point in history the saints in Christ and Christ in the saints are going to rise up and successfully reassert and reestablish free sovereign states and Bible-based Christianity, and in doing so they are going to utterly, totally, and completely defeat the demonically inspired vision, reality, and deception of tyrannical one-world government and phony one-world religion.

This is literal warfare, but it is **not** physical warfare. Rather, it is spiritual, intellectual, and enlightenment warfare against demonic deception and evil that has taken over all of the governments of this world and has taken over almost all of the churches. And in this warfare in Revelation 19 Christ in the saints and the saints in Christ prevail, and the next chapter of Revelation, Revelation 20, says Satan is bound for a thousand years, which seems to indicate that all demons who were reigning over planet Earth with their deceptions, confusions, and evil are also going to be thrown into the bottomless pit with time, if not immediately.

In truth, the victory over the demons' tyrannical one-world government and phony one-world religion seems not only possible, but probable. Why? Because the tyrannical one-world government and the phony one-world religion are such obvious politically correct nonsense. In fact, they are based on absurd, upside-down Orwellian silliness of the first order. (See the booklet "UNDERSTANDING Alternative Political Universes.")

The saints in Christ and Christ in the saints are about to expose this demonic hooey of Social Justice, positive rights, false agape love, the supposed "God" of all religions, utopian selfless service, moral hedonism inclusion, the false Atonement of Christ, etc., etc., for the outrageous nonsense it is. These things are all to be exposed as a false moral superiority and a false enlightenment. One can only say "up is down" and "good is bad" for so long, and then the whole thing falls apart, and the same is true of saying "hedonism is good" and "moral virtue is evil, bigoted, and so forth" or that "Socialist Justice is good" and "classical Justice is evil and exploitive," etc., as we have done in the West since the 1960s.

The Marriage Supper of the Lamb
However, before the saints in Christ and Christ in the saints burst from heaven, so to speak, to expose these

demonic deceptions and falsehoods, there is in Revelation 19 the Marriage Supper of the Lamb.

This passage also has great spiritual literal reality, but in my opinion we should, again, not see it as a literal occurrence where all the saints are physically in heaven at a wedding ceremony to Christ Himself. However, the actual spiritual reality remains: in the Church Age the Church is said to be betrothed or pledged to Christ (and so sees herself) and in the Kingdom Era the Church is said to be the married wife of Christ (and so sees herself), and thus the saints share the throne with Him in doing Just and Righteous governments throughout the world. So, when and where is this point of marriage vow transition and of self-understanding for the Church?

My personal opinion is this involves several things. First and foremost, it is an actual spiritual maturity and depth of spiritual experience with Christ in our hearts as the standard reality of the faith of the whole Body of Christ in a way that did not exist as a general condition (outside of some of the great saints) in the Church Age. And, further, Christianity is understood explicitly as a covenant vow commitment, as in today's Evangelical Christianity with its covenant-like "I do" Sinner's Prayer.

This, in my view, means that the Evangelical Christianity all the churches openly embrace in the Kingdom Era is a notch up, so to speak, in depth, completeness, commitment, and spiritual experience in our hearts, but it is the same basic Christianity come of age. By this I mean Kingdom Era Christianity is going to be not only more spiritually mature and intimate with Christ but openly more **complete** in doing a **Whole Counsel of the Kingdom of God Christianity** as **the norm** of all churches for **the Kingdom Era.**

Whole Counsel of the Kingdom Christianity
Only a Whole Counsel Christianity can defeat the tyrannical one-world government with its worldwide Socialist Justice agenda as a supposed good and at the same time defeat the false one-world religion as a supposed higher enlightenment.

Today, most denominations even when they have few errors or corruptions are generally far from complete in even attempting to do a Whole Counsel of the Kingdom of God. In antiquity the great Saint Augustine made a shot at a Whole Counsel Christianity of the Kingdom, and he set the standard that stands to this day. In modern times the same can be said of John Locke and C. S. Lewis. But Locke, Lewis and Augustine are rare exceptions in doing a Whole Counsel of the Kingdom Christianity. They were not inerrant most people would say, but they were pretty close to it, and they gave us a basis to work from as numerous people are now doing in recent years.

This means most Christianity of the Church Age, even if solidly based on the Bible, was deficient concerning a Whole Counsel of the Kingdom, and much Christianity had at least some defective aspects, sometimes quite serious, such as those that led to the Protestant Reformation. Finally, and this is the important point for Revelation chapter 19, a Marriage Supper of the Lamb Christianity or, that is to say, a Whole Counsel of the Kingdom of God Christianity is necessary to successfully confront, expose, and defeat the demonic deceptions and evil of tyrannical one-world government and phony one-world religion.

Not to be a funny guy here but this is why we must have a Whole Counsel Christianity that commits the saints in covenant vow as in marriage or joining an army **before** the battle of Revelation 19 and not after as we might tend to think we would have **after** the victory. Basically we, as the saints in Christ, are all to be in covenant vow commitment to Christ with a **mature** and **complete** Christianity that can and will accomplish the victory we seek in the final spiritual battle for planet Earth, that is, the victory of utterly, totally, and completely defeating the demonic deceptions and evil of tyrannical one-world government and phony one-world religion.

The World PEACE Plan
In my book *The World PEACE Plan* I try to outline a Whole Counsel of the Kingdom of God Christianity that will accomplish this and that will then go on to serve as a more complete Christianity for a Kingdom Era for a Church that sees itself as spiritually wed to

Christ, somewhat as a spiritually mature equals (as "little christs" as Lewis said), being married *and* sharing the throne with Him quite literally in the realm of the spirit in doing Just and Righteous government in all the nations of the world in the Kingdom Era.

I do not claim to have a corner on the market with this. Numerous people in recent years are and have been pursuing a similar idea to a Whole Counsel of the Kingdom of God Christianity in order for the saints to be successful for the Kingdom in our time, though they do not to my knowledge use "Whole Counsel" terminology but their efforts tend to amount to the same thing.

I am thinking specifically of James Kennedy's efforts to construct a complete two track Christianity of **evangelism** and **cultural mandate** to "reclaim" the nation for Christ in the realm of the spirit. And since Kennedy there are the various Seven Mountain ministries and so-called New Apostolic Reformation ministries, for example, and there are also various binding and loosing ministries, all of which I outline in *The World PEACE Plan* where I try to give as best I can what I see to be most of the various major aspects of a Whole Counsel of the Kingdom of God Christianity for our our time based on the teachings of Jesus, the New Testament, and the Bible generally concerning the Christian cosmology, the Old and New Covenants, salvation, prophecy fulfillment, and good government for the nations worldwide.

Basically the goal of a Whole Counsel of the Kingdom Christianity is twofold: true worship of God in Spirit and Truth in religion along with doing Just and Righteous government in true statesmanship for the common good when one is voting or active in politics. The implications of this for all Christians throughout the world should be obvious.

In all nations where Christians can they **must** vote against **all** globalist candidates of one-world government and one-world religion. In America that would be any and all Democrats and in Britain that would be any and all Labour Party candidates because these are the two political parties promoting the globalist agenda as their very reason for being whether it is in the issue of Social Justice or in the related issues of open borders, radical multiculturalism, false positive human rights, agape love as lawlessness, utopian selfless service or we all supposedly worship the same God but by a different name, and so on.

These politicians are misguided and deceived globalist Social Justice Warriors whether in the Democratic Party or Labour Party (or in Social Democrat parties more generally), and they have successfully pulled off their globalist Socialist Justice agenda for at least the last 50 or so years in the US and UK, but (praise God, not Satan Allah) their days of triumph and winning political battles are now coming to a close! May we so pray to the true God of heaven in the name of our Lord and Savior Jesus Christ!

The Two Components of Victory
There are two separate issues involved in getting the final victory of Revelation 19 over the demonic deceptions and evil of tyrannical one-world Social Justice government to make us all economically equal and over the phony one-world religion that supposedly worships the "God" of all religions, which, in fact, is a demon spirit.

The first thing needed for victory is asking what is *true* salvation in Spirit and Truth? It is accepting the atoning work of Christ for one's self personally for one's sins so that one can be reconciled to God as one invites Christ into one's heart in order to have the spiritual experience of Jesus in one's heart and in order to enter into the Abba Father relationship with the Creator of the entire universe.

The second thing we need for victory is one must come to understand the difference between a good classical Justice as the point of good government *versus* the evil of its opposite, namely, globalist Social Justice to make us all equal and to end all nation-states and to open all borders and so forth. Thinking the globalist Social Justice agenda and all that goes with it (such as radical multiculturalism, agape love as lawlessness, etc.) is a good is a demonic deception, and in truth the globalist Social Justice agenda of the United Nations is a self-evident evil to anyone who has not been ensnared by demonic deception and doctrines of devils as supposedly both true and good when in fact they are neither; they are false and evil.

The Ensnarement of Devils
In the last verses of 2 Timothy 2 Paul instructs Timothy to patiently reason with confused people who are in demonic deception, and in love, one is to patiently teach and correct such people that they may come to their senses and escape the devil's ensnarement and captivity in false teaching. The degree this involves actual demon possession is debated but not the self-evident reality of demonic "ensnarement."

The Left has, in fact, had an agenda in the churches and schools for the past 70 years to create Social Justice Warriors and hence Social Justice voters. They do this by repeating over and over that globalist Social Justice is a good and that classical nation-states with traditional Liberty and Justice for all are either an evil or they are something whose time has past for those who are truly educated, enlightened, progressive, and even loving.

This way when people come to espouse, promote, and vote for the globalist Social Justice agenda they think they are really figuring things out in their confusions, and they think that they are on the right side of history, etc. But, in truth, they understand *neither* good government with Liberty and Justice for all and equal rights for all based on the moral Laws of Nature and of Nature's God Wisely applied by the statesman legislator for the common good **nor** do they understand true Christianity and its history, and this is important because one does **not** have to be an apostate, Democratic or Labour Party member to be a globalist Social Justice Warrior.

A Social Justice Warrior is **anybody** who thinks in their head that the globalist Social Justice agenda is truly a good idea, and they have then taken to heart the false good of the globalist Social Justice agenda. From there they start espousing its nonsense and running for office on it because they have become not just demonically confused in their minds but demonically energized in their hearts or spirits. This does not necessarily make one an evil person, it makes one a victim (of demons), says Paul correctly to Timothy. And it does not matter if it is the Republican W Bush or the Democrat Barack Obama, both were globalist Social Justice Warriors for open borders, amnesty, globalism and so forth, and they both ran for office promoting, in one way or another, a politically correct agenda of one-world government **and** one-world religion to, in effect, merge Christianity and Islam.

Both Bush and Obama promoted the Social Justice entitlement state of phony utopian positive rights, and both were open borders, open immigration, and open amnesty guys, and hence, both were radical multicultural guys, and both were big time one-world religion guys. And though W Bush was personally trusting in Christ for his salvation that did not make him immune to embracing and promoting the demonic errors of one-world religion.

How many speeches did both Bush and Obama give praising Islam and equating it to Christianity and equating Allah to Jehovah?   Both gave these speeches of politically correct religious nonsense and absurdities endlessly, and anyone who objected was said to be an uneducated bigot and an Islamophobe and so forth.

The the strict Islam of Sharia in the unholy Koran (which not all Muslims practice) is an overtly evil thing, period. And to say otherwise is politically correct silliness, but it is extremely serious silliness and to make such ridiculous claims is an overt disqualification for holding any political office by any rational standard.

Further, whether strict Islam is an evil or not, Christianity and Islam are two different religions, and they worship two different Gods, namely, Allah and Jehovah. To my knowledge Allah has always in the West been seen to be a demonic spirit until recent years, but that inconvenient truth cannot be spoken today without being attacked. This is not a value judgment, and it is a free country, and one can worship a demonic spirit if one wishes, but let's get the facts straight. Maybe Satan or any demon worship is a good thing, maybe it is not. Maybe we should have a public debate?

It is only the demonically ensnared and inspired one-world religion people who think all religions worship the same God by a different name or that Allah and Jehovah are one and the same Being. This is not only not true, it is absurd, it is delusional and demonically so. But for the globalist Social Justice Warriors like Bush and Obama these religious outrageous absurdities are considered true, good and brilliant and loving and so forth just as all of the open borders, radical multiculturalism stuff is. Certainly Christians need to speak out and try (as Paul instructs us) to bring the globalist Social Justice Warriors to their senses, and Christians need to expose the false agape love as lawlessness and tolerance, etc., of the apostate Laodicean church as actually being Gnostic demonic and even the essence of anti-Christ and certainly not Christian.

And more than this Christians need to be praying as Jesus instructed us that the Evil One would be restricted and that we are delivered from him in our personal lives and in the society at large so that the Kingdom can come on Earth. And, further, if we are entering the fulfillment of Revelation 19, this would mean it is time to start praying that the deliverance is permanent and that all demons be bound in the bottomless pit, that is, assuming Revelation 20 is referring to all demons and not just to the head demon, Satan himself.

In short, getting the victory over the demonic, hedonist, tyrannical, Social Justice globalist agenda of one-world government and over the outrageously ridiculous one-world religion will mean defeating the last great demonic deception concerning good government and true religion. Once these two things have been exposed for what they are, and once they have been thoroughly defeated and banished from planet Earth for a thousand years, we can then proceed to set up Just and Righteous governments worldwide and to do true worship of God in Spirit and Truth in all the nations. The worldwide deplorables' movement of free and sovereign states led politically by one Donald J. Trump has clearly begun this process for all those with eyes to see.

Enter one Donald J. Trump

The question of all history is did Brexit and the election of Trump mean a temporary delay in the worldwide completion of the globalist Social Justice agenda of the Democrats in the US and of the Labour Party in the UK, *or* were Brexit and Trump's victory mortal blows to the globalist agenda marking the beginning of the end for those two political parties and for all of their demonically inspired hopes and dreams for one-world government and one-world religion for all mankind on planet Earth for the next thousand years? Time will tell no doubt. But if the prophecies of Revelation 19 are true, you can kiss good-bye Social Justice globalism and all of its demonic silliness and supposed moral superiority.

As a practical matter, why are the Democrats and Labour going to lose in the US and the UK? The answer is they are both inherently Social Justice globalist of **a UN variety**, and they never debate the substance of any of their opponents' policy positions or of Trump's policy positions, whether on trade, immigration, the wall, the economy, bad treaties, judicial appointments, climate change, Islam, and so forth. All they do is obstruct, name-call, slander, and conduct seemingly endless phony investigations, prosecutions or witch hunts, which in the US the DOJ and FBI have zero legal statutory authority to do.

At the same time globalists in the Republican Party in the US and globalists in the Conservative Party in the UK will tend to fall away in history as out of touch, irrelevant and unqualified for office because they are, in reality, Republican and Conservative "in name only." These people are truly tragically confused campers, one might say, and they are sometimes called RINOs (Republican in name only) or possibly even CINOs (Conservative in name only), and they tend to be corporate globalists of **an EU variety** as we saw in the US in the two Bush presidencies.

Note: technically, in the UK the "Conservative Party" is the old "Tory Party," which means, in US lingo, roughly traditionalist and not "conservative" in a more ideological sense as we tend to use the term in the states and as we use the term "conservative" to describe a Churchill or a Thatcher. Having said this, technically, the US Republican Party is also not specifically "conservative" historically, but rather it is based on the republican principles of good government as espoused by Abraham Lincoln and set forth in Americans founding documents. The practical implications of this is the Republican and Conservative parties in the US and UK, respectively, tend to be divided between globalists and non-globalists, while the Democratic and Labour parties are almost exclusively globalists in the manner of an H. G. Wells and FDR and of Social Democrat parties more generally.

In any case, regardless, with time and in coming elections as all the fallacies and problems come out with globalism and its false one-world government (of one form or another), the saints in Christ and Christ in the saints will, in fact, presumably achieve the total victory outlined in Revelation 19 over the demonic deceptions of both one-world government as well as its enabling and false one-world religion. Who would have ever dreamed or guessed such a thing just a few short years ago?

===

Other booklets on the Reign of Christ in this UNDERSTANDING Series:

UNDERSTANDING Prophecy Fulfillment:
The Great Apostasy, Babylon, Mystery Babylon & the Reign of Christ

This little booklet gives an overview of the central major prophecies concerning the possible soon coming Reign of Christ. Specifically these are the prophecies of the Great Apostasy, Babylon, Mystery Babylon, and the man of lawlessness. These prophecies are seen as fulfilled in the false millennial visions of Marx and of the New World Order of UN Agenda 21 and Agenda 2030 and in the Liberal World Council of Churches.

UNDERSTANDING All Bible Prophecy:
Genesis to Revelation

This booklet holds that all prophecy should be interpreted in terms of the larger story of the Bible and the larger story of the Christian cosmology from the Creation to the Final Judgment, and this is especially the case for the book of Revelation.

UNDERSTANDING Globalism:
What is the "New World Order"?

This booklet looks at what "globalism" is generally and at the related topic of a "New World Order" that actually has *very* specific definitions and formulations that are often not well-known.

UNDERSTANDING Revelation 19:
Victory over One-World Government and One-World Religion

Revelation 19 though very controversial is actually very straightforward. The saints in a Marriage Supper of the Lamb move into a new more mature, intimate, and complete relationship with Christ, and then the saints in Christ and Christ in the saints completely and totally defeat the evils of one-world government and one-world religion. Simple enough when you get right down to it.

UNDERSTANDING Statesmanship
Classical Justice *versus* Social Justice

Probably no two notions are more misunderstood as well as more necessary to understand in our time than classical Justice and Social Justice. This booklet looks at the history of these two terms and how one stands for the Justice of statesmanship for doing the common good and the other for the injustice of special interest groups and wealth redistribution as a false human right for economic equality.

UNDERSTANDING Alternative
Political Universes:
The Natural Revelation & Self-Evident Truths

For some folks as Jefferson and the American founders, the Natural Law or so-called Higher Moral Law is a self-evident truth, but for others with a reprobate mind and no common sense, this is not the case at all. These modern-day people who have lost their common sense are just as the ancient Epicureans (atheist hedonists) while modern-day Liberals are just as ancient Gnostics with their false enlightenment and false morality. Understand these things, and you will pretty well understand Alternative Political Universes.

UNDERSTANDING Illegal Immigration:
The Wall and All It Stands For

"The Wall" of Donald Trump stands for many larger issues from exposing hypocrisy among professional politicians to ending globalism, open borders, and the often total lawlessness of our time. Lawlessness of the Liberal and atheist-humanist is, in fact, the spirit of anti-Christ.

UNDERSTANDING The Whole Counsel of the Kingdom:
The Central Message of Jesus and Paul

Both Jesus and Paul preached a Whole Counsel of the Kingdom message, but this is not a generally well-known truth. This booklet looks at the concept of a Whole Counsel of the Kingdom Christianity and what it entails, namely, true worship of God in Spirit and Truth as well as Just and Righteous government.

UNDERSTANDING Spiritual Warfare:
Satan as a Roaring Lion

Scripture tells us that Satan goes about like a roaring lion seeking whom he may devour, but this is generally not a very understood warning, and tragically many people, if not devoured completely, get an arm or leg eaten (so to speak). To be forewarned is to be forearmed. This booklet deals with ways to recognize and deal with demons.

===

All of the above booklets are part of a series on key issues of our time on the Reign of Christ at
www.ashiningcityonahill.org
www.reignofchrist.org

All of the above booklets are put together is a single **Volume I** called

UNDERSTANDING
The Reign of CHRIST
The One Big Issue of Our Time
Volume I

This Volume I of all the above booklets together as well as all of the above booklets separately are available at **amazon.com**